AUTHOR'S BIO.

W. Monson was born in 1925 at home on the farm during a chilly day in North Dakota. She was the 3rd of 9 children. Her grandparents were immigrants from Russia. They came to the United States in 1905. Her great-great-grandparents had immigrated from Prussia to Russia in the early 1800's.

Life was not easy for their large family. W. Monson worked in the fields and milked cows. She carried pail after pail of water for drinking, cleaning, and washing clothes. In the winter she walked to the little school house 5 miles away. As a teenager she began to understand that Jesus is her personal Savior.

When she was 17 years of age W. Monson moved to sunny California. A friend invited her along one Sunday morning to church. It was there she was confirmed and baptized. Moving back to North Dakota, she married a Christian man, Lowell, her husband of 63 years. They raised their children with Christian guidance. Every night, at 9:00 P.M., she and all six of her children and often her children's friends were called together in the home for "prayer-time." The Bible was read, a devotional studied, and the entire group took part in prayer.

Sunday church service and Sunday school were seldom missed. W. Monson taught Sunday school for nearly 20 years and helped lead the woman's Bible study. She spent many hours of her time testifying through Lutheran lay renewals.

W. Monson's trust is in the Lord. Her hope, faith, joy, and love have inspired family and friends and challenged them to seek a deeper relationship with God. Her sincere desire is that the poems in this book touch every heart that reads them.

TO MAN FROM GOD, Vol. 2

Holy Spirit Inspired Prayers,

Poems, Lyrics, Raps, and

Phonemic Expressions of Love

by

W. Monson,
C. Erwin,
and M. Monson,
Mother and Daughters

VISION
PUBLISHING
NORTH DAKOTA
U. S. A.

Scripture taken from the New King James Version.
Copyright © 1982 by Thomas Nelson, Inc. Used by permission.
All rights reserved.

To Man from God, Vol. 2
Holy Spirit Inspired Prayers, Poems, Lyrics,
Raps, and Phonemic Expressions of Love

ISBN 978-0-9835799-1-5

Copyright © 2014 W. Monson, C. Erwin, and M. Monson
First Edition

Editor: Sausha Marie Renfro-Stone

Vision Publishing
North Dakota
U.S.A.

Dedications by Permission

Printed in the United States of America. All rights reserved. No parts of this book may be reproduced or copied in any format or by any method unless written permission is obtained from the authors.

We would like to dedicate
this book
to
the loving memory
of Lowell A. Monson.

It is beyond our ability to explain
how much he has given unselfishly
to
his family,
his friends,
and society in general.

Lowell A. Monson holds a diligent vigil among the Saints.

A special thank you to Sharon Opdahl
for her kindness,
her ability to express her faith,
her willingness to witness for the Lord,
and the encouragement
she has offered
to all of those who seek her counsel,
as did the authors
of this book.

All Original Artwork

Illustrations by
Zelma Shapley, Shannon Little Dog, and M. Monson

INTRODUCTION

<u>How do I know?</u>
by Gloria Van Dyke

Thanks be to God
I've been set free.
How do I know?
Because He died for me.

Thanks be to God
My sins are forgiven.
How do I know?
Because He has risen.

Thanks be to God
I've been given a new start.
How do I know?
Because He lives in my heart.

CONTENTS

The Words I Say	1
His Awesome Love	3
God Gave You to Us	5
Rock of Love	7
Power	9
Love Is	11
Grown Too Soon	13
Go Tell Everyone	15
He Bore the Sins of All Mankind	17
No More Pain	19
The Love of Easter	21
The Congregation's Prayer	23
Truthful Gems	25
My Dearest Friend	27
Truthful Gems	29
I Love Your Gospel, Lord	31
Parent's Prayer	33

CONTENTS (Continued...)

You Can Pray	35
What Love You Have for Me	37
Jesus Will Lead Me	39
Brother, We Pray	41
Holy Passageway	43
As Far the East is From the West	45
Reach Down to Me	47
Phonemic Expression of Love - Father	49
Phonemic Expression of Love - Mother	51
A Mother's Love	53
Faith	55
Jesus, My Light	57
His Blood, His Joy	59
Calmed	61
God, You are Everything	63
Truthful Gems	65
Just Say Jesus	67
Oh, Dear Lord of Light	69

CONTENTS (Continued…)

Gap Rappers' Rap	71
Biblical Maturity	77
Heaven's Little Angels	79
I Thank You, Lord	81
Love So Pure, So Free	83
Loving Grace	85
Fulfilled	87
The Dark Hour	89
God's Love for Me	91
Truthful Gems	93
True Friendship	95
Oh, God, Keep My Heart	97
The Guest	99
God Whispers	101
Lord	103
In the Light of the Spirit	105
The End	107
Truthful Gems	109

THE WORDS I SAY

Every idle word that
I speak without relent
Must be accounted for in heaven,
When I stand in God's judgment.

With the blood of Jesus
I lean in heaven's court,
Intently clasping my salvation,
Grasping Jesus for support.

My defense is Jesus.
He forgives and saves me.
For God does not desire sacrifice,
As He desires mercy.

"His Awesome Love" is dedicated to all people who by faith know that Jesus is the Son of God, the Christ, and our Savior, and to all people in all nations who are seeking the Messiah.

Isaiah 53:5-6
⁵ But He *was* wounded for our transgressions,
He *was* bruised for our iniquities;
The chastisement for our peace *was* upon Him,
And by His stripes we are healed.
⁶ All we like sheep have gone astray;
We have turned, every one, to his own way;
And the LORD has laid on Him the iniquity of us all.

Isaiah 57:15
¹⁵ For thus says the High and Lofty One
 Who inhabits eternity, whose name *is* Holy:
 "I dwell in the high and holy *place,*
 With him *who* has a contrite and humble spirit,
 To revive the spirit of the humble,
 And to revive the heart of the contrite ones.

HIS AWESOME LOVE
by W. Monson

How awesome I, a sinner low,
Who in the mire of self, yet trod,
Though contrite heart, on bended knee,
Should dare approach the throne of God.

Oft' in my mind my Lord I see
Still bleeding on that wooden frame,
And, oh! To think He died for me;
He bore that cross of hate and shame.

Then I can hear old Satan laugh
From in the cesspool of his hell,
Each time a precious child of God
Lies struggling, dying where he fell.

That one whom Jesus called His own,
Now led by Satan, gone astray,
Has turned away from such pure love,
For intercession, Lord, I pray.

Oh, stir in me a love for all,
So I a helping hand may hold,
When I see someone trodden down,
To lift that struggling, dying soul.

"God Gave You to Us" is dedicated to the loving parents of the Monson family and to all parents who have taken responsibility for children, because they love them.

Exodus 20:12
[12] " Honor your father and your mother, that your days may be long upon the land which the LORD your God is giving you.

Ephesians 6:1-3
[1] Children, obey your parents in the Lord, for this is right. [2] *"Honor your father and mother,"* which is the first commandment with promise: [3] *"that it may be well with you and you may live long on the earth."*[a]

GOD GAVE YOU TO US
by C. Erwin and M. Monson

Oh, Mother so kind,
With your hair brown and white,
We remember the way
You kissed us goodnight,
The sweet smile you wore,
And the tears that you wiped,
The Word of God that you read
To teach us wrong from right.

Oh, Father so kind,
With your dear, shiny crown,
We remember the way
You took us around.
A smile for a friend,
A nod for another,
The good example you set
Of love for your brother.

Oh, parents so kind,
Twined inside God's design,
With two caring hearts,
Given us over time.
We do not ask why,
Though we found it was true,
We were given to know love
When God gave us to you.

"Rock Of Love" is dedicated to the memory of John Sundquist, who is now a resident in heaven, and to his wife, Audrey Sundquist, Valley City, North Dakota. Family and friends have sincerely known the consistent support of John and Audrey, who have guided them with wisdom and love.

Matthew 7:24-25
24 "Therefore whoever hears these sayings of Mine, and does them, I will liken him to a wise man who built his house on the rock: 25 and the rain descended, the floods came, and the winds blew and beat on that house; and it did not fall, for it was founded on the rock.

ROCK OF LOVE
by W. Monson, C. Erwin, and M. Monson

Father, grant my grip may be
Firm upon the rock that stands.
Though winds may buffet,
Clouds may roll,
Yet safe in Thee is stayed my soul.
Great awe have I for Thy commands.
I rest me in Thy loving hands.

Mount Zion's Chief Cornerstone,
Tells us to love each other,
Then from the right side
Of Thy throne,
Thy healing power is made known,
With earnest prayer for another,
Faith and truth
Shine in my brother.

As the cover of the snow
Quilts the roots, so warm a lee,
Now safe am I, for Thou art near,
Thy grace my shelter without fear.
My life, my all, I yield to Thee,
For Thou art everything to me.

"Power" is dedicated to Marlowe Monson, a man who walks boldly with the authority of God's Word.

Ezekiel 8:2
² Then I looked, and there was a likeness, like the appearance of fire—from the appearance of His waist and downward, fire; and from His waist and upward, like the appearance of brightness, like the color of amber.

Luke 3:16
¹⁶ John answered, saying to all, "I indeed baptize you with water; but One mightier than I is coming, whose sandal strap I am not worthy to loose. He will baptize you with the Holy Spirit and fire.

POWER
by M. Monson

Throw some fire down from heaven,
Let it burn into my heart.
Let it roll off my tongue.
Let it light up the dark.
There is power in the fire,
It grows stronger by the hour.
Let me walk with the power of the Lord!

Praise the glory of the Savior,
Let it cheer up my spirit.
Let it sing from my soul.
Let the whole world hear it!
There is power praising Jesus,
It grows stronger by the hour.
Let me praise with the power of the Lord!

Send Your prophets down on chariots.
They will whirl with the wind.
Let this be the power,
That we all enter in.
There is fire with the prophets.
Let me streak up in the sky.
Let me fly the chariots on high!

"Love Is" is dedicated to Vicky Justesen Hlubek, Erskine, Minnesota, who chose to follow God's calling of ministering to people's health.

2 Thessalonians 1:11-12
[11] Therefore we also pray always for you that our God would count you worthy of *this* calling, and fulfill all the good pleasure of *His* goodness and the work of faith with power, [12] that the name of our Lord Jesus Christ may be glorified in you, and you in Him, according to the grace of our God and the Lord Jesus Christ.

LOVE IS
by W. Monson

Love is ecstasy,
Love is mystery,
Love is history,
God is love.

Love is never
Boastful,
Or arrogant, or rude.
Jesus showed
His love,
When He fed
The multitude.

Love is music fine.
Love is grace divine.
Love makes
Jesus mine.
God is love.

Love is
Always helpful
To everyone, I find,
Jesus showed His love
When He healed
The beggar blind.

Love is sins forgiven.
Love makes life
Worth livin'.
Love came down
From heaven.
God is love.

Love comes
In the morning,
Or when I lay and toss.
Jesus showed
His love,
When He died upon
The cross.

Love is ecstasy.
Love is mystery.
Love is history.
God is love.

"Grown Too Soon" is dedicated from W. Monson to her daughter, C. Erwin, a woman who sings beautiful praises to uplift the name of Jesus.

Psalm 52:8-9
8 But I am like an olive tree
   flourishing in the house of God;
I trust in God's unfailing love
   for ever and ever.
9 For what you have done I will always praise you in the presence of your faithful people. And I will hope in your name,
   for your name is good.

GROWN TOO SOON
by W. Monson

Come back!
My heart cries out,
I cannot let you go.
When you were
Just a babe
I bathed your soft,
New skin,
And brushed your
Silken
Hair.
Your eyes
So trusting,
Looked at me,
And oh,
My heart
Beat in
My breast
A thank you cry
To God!
Come back!
My heart cried out
As off to school you went,
So full of eagerness,
So free from care,
Some unkind words,
Some pulling hair, but
Mostly love and friends.
You weathered
All the storms,
And God, so kind,
Healed all your pains.

Come back!
My heart
Cried out again,
As teenage challenge came.
With pretty clothes
And dancing toes,
Your courage never faltering.
With father's strength
And mother's prayers,
You marched
On straight ahead…
God quieted
My fears.

Now, again
My heart cries out,
Come back!
Come back!
I cannot let you go,
The current
Is too strong,
The wind that blows
Will sweep you
Far away.
Oh, God,
My child
Has gone from me
Into a distant day,
And though the pain
I scarce can bear,
This is
As it should be…
God keep you in His care.

"Go Tell Everyone" is dedicated to Pastor Terry Monson and his wife, Linda, of the Bethel Lutheran Church, Rogers, North Dakota and Our Saviour's Lutheran Church, Dazey, North Dakota. The Word of God's salvation is expressed within these churches in a kind and caring manner, giving evidence that the love of Jesus Christ is spoken through the power of the Holy Spirit.

Isaiah 52:8
8 Your watchmen shall lift up *their* voices,
With their voices they shall sing together;
For they shall see eye to eye
When the LORD brings back Zion.

Daniel 5:14
14 I have heard of you, that the Spirit of God *is* in you, and *that* light and understanding and excellent wisdom are found in you.

GO TELL EVERYONE
by C. Erwin

I had suffered every day as a prisoner of sin,
Swayed by this world that I was born in.
I was searching to be free from such soulful misery.
Who then would care to save me? Is there anyone?

(Refrain)
Seek and you will find Him.
Knock and the door will open.
Go ask of the Father, child, through His Holy Son.
When you pray to Jesus,
And feel God's anointing come,
Don't hesitate or wait,
Go tell everyone!

I was hiding every day as a prisoner of lies,
Breaking down in sorrow heaving sighs.
I was forever dying,
Tears were streaming from my eyes.
Who then could hear me crying? Is there anyone?
(Repeat Refrain)

I was running every day as a prisoner in flight,
Lost in the dark, racing out of sight.
I was sinking down inside,
Where there's no place left to hide.
Who would come and take my side? Is there anyone?
(Repeat Refrain)

"He Bore the Sins of All Mankind" is dedicated to Frank and Carol Faulkner, Chandler, Arizona, who are devoted and compassionate friends of Jesus.

Galatians 5:22-23
22 But the fruit of the spirit is love, joy, peace, longsuffering, kindness, goodness, faithfulness, 23 gentleness, self-control. Against such there is no law.

HE BORE THE SINS OF ALL MANKIND
by W. Monson

Holy Word
Came down from heaven,
Taking on the flesh of man.
Son of God,
By grace was given,
Lead to slaughter
Like a lamb.

(Refrain)
He bore the sins
Of all mankind,
Yet, no fault in Him
They find.

Jesus left his home in glory,
Where the saints
His praises sang.
On this earth
Man did abhor Him,
"Crucify!" their
Voices rang.
(Repeat Refrain)

Willingly to be the ransom,
Jesus, lowly,
Meek and mild,
Bore the cross
To dark Golgotha,
He, the Father's Holy Child.
(Repeat Refrain)

Bowed down before
That crimson cross,
Stripped of all
My pomp and pride.
I heard Him softly
Call my name,
As the blood
Flowed from His side.
(Repeat Refrain)

Easter morning,
Bright and early,
Found the Savior
Undefiled.
That no grave
Could ever hold Him,
He has come
To claim His child.
(Repeat Refrain)

Such wondrous
Joy, beyond compare,
Has me praising
Him in song.
Christ was dead and
Now is living,
Praise Him! Christians,
All day long.
(Repeat Refrain)

"No More Pain" is dedicated to Brandon Krenz, Lewisville, Texas, and to all people who have lost loved ones on this earth, but know that they will one day see them again in heaven's eternal home.

Revelations 21:4
4 And God will wipe away every tear from their eyes, there shall be no more death, nor sorrow, nor crying. There shall be no more pain, for the former things have passed away."

NO MORE PAIN
by W. Monson

On this earth, our pain is great,
And we cannot explain,
Why our heavenly Father
Would allow us so much pain.

    He tells us He is with us,
        While we are on this earth.
            He seeks us with His Spirit,
                From the moment
                    Of our birth.

                    We know
            That God is saddened,
            When people turn away.
            Within His Word He calls us,
            And He teaches us to pray.

                So let us not
                Grow weary,
            Nor ever count it loss,
            For Jesus, too, did suffer,
            While He hung upon the cross.

One day life will be different,
The pain will be no more,
As we see the Savior's face,
When we reach a brighter shore.

"The Love of Easter" is dedicated to Diane Meehan, Justin, Texas, a woman whose love for others is shown in her kind actions and deeds.

1 Corinthians 15:20-22
[20] But now Christ is risen from the dead, *and* has become the first fruits of those who have fallen asleep. [21] For since by man *came* death, by Man also *came* the resurrection of the dead. [22] For as in Adam all die, even so in Christ all shall be made alive.

THE LOVE OF EASTER
by W. Monson

Look up to the Lord
From where comes our help,
Our courage, joy and salvation.
See our God above,
Who in His infinite love
Has so given
His own Son
To heal the sins of His creation.

Look up to Him lest
In this world we fail to recognize
His love to earth,
To win our crown,
And give to Him His due renown.
He who died has rose to life.
And we celebrate His timely birth.

Look up with open eyes
And contrite heart to see
The empty cross
Now glow,
To show in earthly sight,
That man might see God's light,
There on died the Lamb,
When from His wounds
His blood did flow.

"The Congregation's Prayer" is dedicated to Reverend Jim Black and his wife, Lisa, of the First Baptist Church, Valley City, North Dakota and to the congregation of the First Baptist Church. Within and throughout this church there are deep and abiding spiritual gifts of love for family, for friends, and for neighbors.

Psalms 104:3-4
3 He lays the beams of His upper chambers in the waters,
    Who makes the clouds His chariot,
    Who walks on the wings of the wind,
4 Who makes His angels spirits,
His ministers a flame of fire.

The CONGREGATION'S PRAYER
by M. Monson

Dear Lord, our heavenly Father,
    From Your Word our hearts will speak,
        On the byways and the highways,
            In the valleys dark and deep.
                Boldly stepping out with Jesus,
              Seeking both the strong and weak.
        Calling for the lost and lonely.
        Going forth to find the sheep.

(1st Refrain)
    Calling to Your sons and daughters,
    Saying children, come to me.
    Come to the Spring of Living Waters,
    Where your blessed eyes will see.

Dear Lord, our heavenly Father,
What You want is our desire.
From the desert to the mountains
Fill us up with heaven's fire.
Testifying to the children,
With Your wind the flames will leap.
Quoting verses from the scriptures,
Going forth to feed the sheep.

    (2nd Refrain)
    Quoting to Your sons and daughters,
    Saying children, you I seek.
    Come to the Spring of Living Waters,
    Where your blessed tongues will speak.

THE CONGREGATION'S PRAYER (Continued...)

Dear Lord, our heavenly Father,
Spread this urgent message on,
Across the rivers, land, and sky,
Where the borders lie beyond.
Gifts we carry from the Spirit,
Gifts too marvelous to keep.
Sharing Jesus with the nations,
Going forth to lead the sheep.

(3rd Refrain)
Sharing with Your sons and daughters,
Sharing as we gather near.
Come to the Spring of Living Waters,
Where your blessed ears will hear.

Truthful Gems

Psalm 100:3
3 Know that the LORD, He *is* God;
It is He *who* has made us, and not we ourselves;[a]
We are His people and the sheep of His pasture.

Zephaniah 3:12
12 I will leave in your midst
A meek and humble people,
And they shall trust in the name of the LORD.

John 4:14
14 but whoever drinks of the water that I shall give him will never thirst. But the water that I shall give him will become in him a fountain of water springing up into everlasting life."

Philippians 4:8
8 Finally, brethren, whatever things are true, whatever things *are* noble, whatever things *are* just, whatever things *are* pure, whatever things *are* lovely, whatever things *are* of good report, if *there is* any virtue and if *there is* anything praiseworthy—meditate on these things.

"Jesus, My Precious Lord" is dedicated sincerely to Henry Middlestead, Valley City, North Dakota and Walter and Dorothy Reinke from Townsend, Montana, and to all the relatives, the nieces, nephews, and grandchildren in the Middlestead family, as they reach out to others with friendship and love.

John 15:11-15
[11] "These things I have spoken to you, that My joy may remain in you, and *that* your joy may be full. [12] This is My commandment, that you love one another as I have loved you. [13] Greater love has no one than this, than to lay down one's life for his friends. [14] You are My friends if you do whatever I command you. [15] No longer do I call you servants, for a servant does not know what his master is doing; but I have called you friends, for all things that I heard from My Father I have made known to you.

JESUS, MY PRECIOUS LORD
by W. Monson and C. Erwin

Who is the dearest friend I have ever known?
Jesus, my precious Lord.
Who has for this sinner such mercy shown?
Jesus, my precious Lord.
He made the earth, the sea and the sky,
Created the birds and taught them to fly,
Yet attends to the needs of all sinners like I.
Jesus, my precious Lord.

Who has filled this sin-darkened world with His light?
Jesus, my precious Lord.
Who is the sorrowing heart's pure delight?
Jesus, my precious Lord.
He is the one so gentle and kind,
Who opened the eyes of the beggar blind.
If we ask, He will open the eyes of our mind.
Jesus, my precious Lord.

Who has walked on this earth and taught us to pray?
Jesus, my precious Lord.
Who lifts our burdens and straightens the way?
Jesus, my precious Lord.
He spoke to the wind and calmed the sea.
His joy and grace are abundantly free.
Through the storms of my life,
He speaks peace unto me.
Jesus, my precious Lord.

JESUS, MY PRECIOUS LORD (Continued…)

Who was hung on the cross of Golgotha's hill?
Jesus, my precious Lord.
Who prayed for the lost as His blood did spill?
Jesus, my precious Lord.
'Tis there on the cross He took my place.
Now all of my sins are covered by grace.

He died for all people, every color and race.
Jesus, my precious Lord.

Who now sits at the right of God's Holy throne?
Jesus, my precious Lord.
Who is coming soon to gather His own?
Jesus, my precious Lord.

He sent His Spirit to guide our ways;
We walk in forgiveness all of our days.
Come and sing with great joy of His glory and praise
Jesus, my precious Lord.

Truthful Gems

Psalm 25:10
10 All the paths of the LORD are mercy and truth, to such as keep His covenant and His testimonies.

Proverbs 16:3
3 Commit your works to the LORD,
And your thoughts will be established.

Isaiah 59:1
1 Behold, the LORD's hand is not shortened,
That it cannot save;
Nor His ear heavy,
That it cannot hear.

Matthew 11:28
28 Come to Me, all you who labor and are heavy laden, and I will give you rest.

James 1:25
25 But he who looks into the perfect law of liberty and continues in it, and is not a forgetful hearer but a doer of the work, this one will be blessed in what he does.

"I Love Your Gospel, Lord" is dedicated to Viola (Dolly) Hoelmer with South Central Adult Services, Valley City, North Dakota. Dolly's life is a testimony for the Gospel. She is devoted to helping others, as she effectively and cheerfully provides outreach services for the elderly.

Ephesians 1:13-14
¹³ In Him you also trusted, after you heard the word of truth, the gospel of your salvation, in whom also, having believed, you were sealed with the Holy Spirit of promise, ¹⁴ who[a] is the guarantee of our inheritance until the redemption of purchased possession, to the praise of His glory.

I LOVE YOUR GOSPEL, LORD
by W. Monson and M. Monson

I love Your Gospel, Lord,
    The Word, Your grace divine,
      That tells me of Your love so pure,
And makes salvation mine.

I love Your Gospel, Lord,
  My help in You, I find,
Your fellowship, the joy of life,
  Your truth in faith designed.

I love Your Gospel, Lord,
My hope that all may hear,
To seek to honor Your great name,
That death is not to fear.

I love Your Gospel, Lord,
Therein I find great peace,
To guide me until Your return,
When sin and sorrow cease.

I love Your Gospel, Lord,
    Your light unto my feet,
      The light that brightens up my way,
And makes my life complete.

"Parent's Prayer" is dedicated to Barnes County, North Dakota, Salvation Army Coordinator, Joseph J. Lunde and his wife, Martee J. who direct and enable a dedicated society of people offering love and hope to others. The prayers of many parents have been answered from contributions collected through God's service, the Salvation Army.

Psalm 6:9
9 **The LORD has heard my supplication;
The LORD will receive my prayer.**

Parent's Prayer
by W. Monson

Precious Jesus,
Only Savior,
Take our children
To Your heart.
Fill them with
Your Holy Spirit.
From Thee -
May they never part.
Instill in them
Your understanding
Of man's lost,
Condition's need.
Open now their eyes
To show them,
By Your undying love,
They're freed.

"You Can Pray" is dedicated to God's beloved woman, Renee Monroe, who with the love of Jesus in her heart, has heard and answered God's call from the time she was a small child.

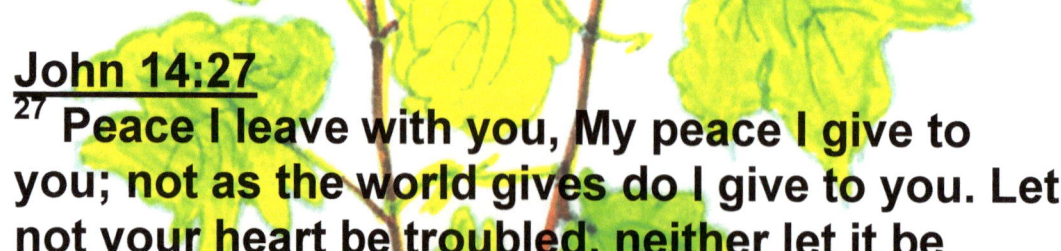

John 14:27
27 **Peace I leave with you, My peace I give to you; not as the world gives do I give to you. Let not your heart be troubled, neither let it be afraid.**

YOU CAN PRAY
by C. Erwin and M. Monson

There is a God, He's watching over you.
His Son is Jesus and He died for you.
I can tell you what my God can do,
I can tell you He can take you through.

    Through a mountain of heartache,
    A hollow of fears,
    An aching of loneliness,
    A fountain of tears.
God will say, "Child! Child! I am calling for you!"
You can pray, "Jesus, I'm falling! Please carry me through!
Through the edge of this longing I cannot let go of,
Lord, take me into Your presence, with Your powerful love."

There is a God, He really loves you, too!
His Son is Jesus, and He died for you.
You can hear Him when He calls you, too.
Hear the message that He has for you!

  You are wanting and waiting
  For a friend that is true.
  Inside of the emptiness
  God will hold unto you.
  God will say, "Child! Child! Hear me calling for you!"
  You can pray, "Jesus, I'm falling! Please carry me through!"
  Through the end of all trouble; From the easing of pain,
  Jesus will come and attend you, when you call on His name.

You can call Him. He will come to you.
With His Spirit He will move with you.
He's the Savior. He will help you through.
His name is Jesus, and He died for you.

"What Love You Have for Me" is dedicated to Lewis W. Renfro, Jr., who reaches out to the society of humanity with patient consideration for all people, as he demonstrates God's service with his willing heart to help others in need.

1 John 4:7
⁷ Beloved, let us love one another, for love is of God; and everyone who loves is born of God and knows God.

WHAT LOVE YOU HAVE FOR ME
by W. Monson and C. Erwin

What love
You have for me,
To bear upon the tree,
The wrath
Of God's own Hand,
That my sin does demand.
You cleansed and
Set me Free,
Unworthy, though I be.

What love
You have for me,
To give me air so free,
To all my burdens share,
And keep me in Your care.
You gave me hands to fold,
And beauty to behold.

What love
You have for me.
My need to grow
You see.
Oh, help me
Bare each pain,
Not bitterly complain,
To do and to endure,
For my salvation's sure.

What love
To hear my cry.
You did not
Pass me by,
But made
My spirit know,
Of how You
Love me so.
Your precious life
You gave,
To sanctify and save.

What love
You have for me.
Now help my eyes
To see,
The needs
Of others, too.
And teach me
What to do,
To ease their
Pain and strife,
Along
The path of life.

"Jesus Will Lead Me" is dedicated to Donald Hilscher, from Trinity, Texas, a man who has the wisdom to establish peace and benefit others by sharing with those who need help.

Acts 20:35
[35] I have shown you in every way, by laboring like this, that you must support the weak. And remember the words of the Lord Jesus, that He said, 'It is more blessed to give than to receive.'"

JESUS WILL LEAD ME
by M. Monson

There is a home in paradise
That God has made for me,
A happy home to keep my soul
Through all eternity.

(Refrain)
Jesus will lead me
Up to His kingdom,
Up to His kingdom,
Where He sits on His throne.
Jesus will lead all who believe Him
Up to His kingdom.
Take up your cross and follow Him home

The life I live on earthly ground
Is just a stopping place.
Heavenly hope to hold unto
Is why I run this race.
(Repeat Refrain)

This race I run, I win by faith,
And love is at my side.
Heavenly guide to keep me safe
From jealousy and pride.
(Repeat Refrain)

I labor hard to help the weak,
With mercy, I believe,
That more blessed am I to give
Then that I should receive.
(Repeat Refrain)

"Brother, We Pray" is dedicated to the memory of Robin Allen Monson and to the families and friends of others who have lost loved ones by self-inflicted wounds.

Galatians 6:2
² Bear one another's burdens, and so fulfill the law of Christ.

BROTHER, WE PRAY
By C. Erwin

Brother, we pray,
When we think of your stay,
And your worth
As you walked on the earth,
Giving out love
From the glow in your heart,
One highly esteemed
Whom God set apart.

You smiled
And beguiled
With light in your eyes,
Hiding a sadness that
Comes with the wise.
More thoughtful
Than most
For others in need,
Their cry out for help
Became your good deed.

Brave and strong, too,
Unafraid of the chore,
Bracing the weight of the cross that you bore.
You lifted the load of friends that you knew,
Hoisting their burdens, you carried them through.

Sadly, we gathered to tell you goodbye,
You left us too soon, and we wondered why.
Brother, we pray, we will see you one day,
Your lessons of love have taught us the way.

"Holy Passageway" is dedicated to Robert Miller, Grandfather, and Pamela Erickson, Granddaughter, Eckelson, North Dakota. They carry in their hearts a special dominion and love for God's animals on this earth.

John 1:51
⁵¹ **And He said to him, "Most assuredly, I say to you, hereafter**[j] **you shall see heaven open, and the angels of God ascending and descending upon the Son of Man."**

John 14:2
² **In My Father's house are many mansions;**[a] **if *it were* not *so,* I would have told you. I go to prepare a place for you.**[b]

HOLY PASSAGEWAY
by M. Monson

Truly, there is only one sin,
That we will never be forgiven,
That will keep us out
Of heaven,
Separated from the living.

If we were to be rejecting
The Holy Spirit's sweet instilling,
Turn our lives to God's electing.
Dear Lord Jesus, find us willing.

We must stand
Upon God's scriptures,
Humbly heeding and committing
Showing love and be forgiving,
Serving others through God's bidding.

The Messiah is projecting,
His saving grace, as He's connecting
Every soul that He's perfecting,
In eternity's directing.

The great love line God is holding,
In Christ's assurance and enfolding,
With the Holy Spirit's filling,
Dear Lord Jesus, keep us willing.

Willing temples
God is filling.
He is filling us that
We may pray.
Praying, "Lead us
Into heaven,
Through Your
Holy **Passageway**."

"As Far as the East is From the West" is dedicated to the Monson family relatives in Jamestown, North Dakota and throughout the state, from Washington to Minnesota, from Texas to Virginia, and from Arizona to South Dakota. The Monson families witness for the love of the Lord our God.

Psalm 103:11-12

11 For as the heavens are high above the earth,
    So **great is His mercy toward those who fear Him;**
12 As far as the east is from the west,
    So **far has He removed our transgressions from us.**

AS FAR AS THE EAST IS FROM THE WEST
by W. Monson and C. Erwin

(Refrain)
As far as the East is from the West
Now all my sin is gone.
I claim the promises of God.
His grace I rest upon.

Saved by the righteousness of Christ,
This doing not my own.
The Son of God who died, now lives,
And for my sin atones.
His body hung upon the tree.
His blood the cleansing power,
Crying, "Father, forgive their sins!"
Deep in His suffering hour.
(Repeat Refrain)

Lord, I come to the empty cross,
Here in repentance kneel,
And thank You for all You have done,
I tell the world You're real.
The joy that overflows my soul,
The awesome gift You give.
Oh, Jesus, Lord, what price You paid,
That now this sinner lives.
(Repeat Refrain)

Oh, people of this world beware,
The time goes swiftly by,
And though the Lord has not returned,
His coming doth draw nigh.
When God proclaims the time fulfilled,
A new age He will bring.
Dear Christians, let us spread His Word,
That all on earth may sing.
(Repeat Refrain)

"Reach Down to Me" is dedicated to faithful fathers among the Lord's creation, who are within all the nations of the world. These are the men who care faithfully for their wives and their children, as did Lowell A. Monson.

Psalms 123:1-2
¹ Unto You I lift up my eyes,
O You who dwell in the heavens.
² Behold, as the eyes of servants look to the hand of their masters,
As the eyes of a maid to the hand of her mistress,
So our eyes look to the Lord our God,
Until He has mercy on us.

Romans 1:5-6
⁵ Through Him we have received grace and apostleship for obedience to the faith among all nations for His name, ⁶ among whom you also are the called of Jesus Christ;

REACH DOWN TO ME
by W. Monson, C. Erwin, and M. Monson

From out of the depth of my soul, Lord, I cry,
Reach down to me.
The rewards of the world have all passed me by.
How can this be?

It is true I have worked all my life long.
I have slaved in the mills with the weak and the strong.
I have prayed in the church and sang praises in song.
I have made many choices and some of them wrong.

From out of the depth of my soul, Lord, I cry,
Reach down to me.
I am tired and sick and blind in one eye.
How can this be?

Faithful and true, I have stayed with my wife.
I have given more than my ten percent tithe.
The pain that I wear cuts like a sharp bladed knife.
I have given my heart to you, Lord, and my life.

From out of the depth of my soul, Lord, I cry,
Reach down to me.
I breathe the last breath from my body and die.
How can this be?

The love of Your promise You send as my guide.
You comfort my spirit in this marvelous ride.
Now I'm gazing in heaven right by your side.
The glories I can see are the reasons I cried,
Reach down to me.

"Father" is dedicated to Lowell A. Monson, who has arrived in his heavenly home. This phonemic expression of love is also dedicated to all fathers in all nations of this world.

Genesis 1:26-27
26 Then God said, "Let Us make man in Our image, according to Our likeness; let them have dominion over the fish of the sea, over the birds of the air, and over the cattle, over all[b] the earth and over every creeping thing that creeps on the earth." 27 So God created man in His *own* image; in the image of God He created him; male and female He created them.

FATHER
by C. Erwin

F Is for the "FONDNESS" always shown to his own. So strong he stands, like an oak, ready to shoulder my burdens. He speaks to me with a gentle tone and helps ease any hurt.

A Is for the "AWE" always felt whenever he is near. His words just right, conveying love and through the years, assurance and affection. On these our relationship stands so always. I know, I can depend on him.

T Is for the "TREAT" it is to listen to him talk. He makes me laugh and the thought occurs: *Time is but a factor to be spent with him*—inspiring and true the hours spent with him. Tumults may arise, yet, he sails right on through with faith and love abounding. Love bears him ever on.

H Is for the "HARMONY" he always seems to bring, causing peace once more to reign as ruler of his house. Suffering, yes, but enduring all, and showing his belief, by putting his trust in God; resulting in a magnificence of character, seldom seen in others—though I've searched.

E Is for the "EMBRACE," the giving of himself. His powerful arms encircling me with pride and emotion. I need his love and strength. So gladly he gives them—enveloping me, securing me—conveying a power of greatness to greatness, God shines through.

R Is for the "RARITY" with which I regard him. Respect is ringing through my soul, tying it to his. Memories cherished of wise advice, my good his greatest concern, even across the way. I pray to God that he knows his child loves him.

He has endeared himself to me!
If only every child could have a father such as he.
Keep him in Your care and watch over him possessively, Dear God.

"Mother" is dedicated to WillaMae Monson, who some refer to a saint here on earth and will arrive someday in her heavenly home. This phonemic expression of love is also dedicated to all mothers in all nations of this world.

Genesis 2:20-23

[20] So Adam gave names to all cattle, to the birds of the air, and to every beast of the field. But for Adam there was not found a helper comparable to him. [21] And the LORD God caused a deep sleep to fall on Adam, and he slept; and He took one of his ribs, and closed up the flesh in its place. [22] Then the rib which the LORD God had taken from man He made into a woman, and He brought her to the man. [23] And Adam said:

"This *is* now bone of my bones
And flesh of my flesh;
She shall be called Woman,
Because she was taken out of Man."

MOTHER
by C. Erwin

M Is for the "MEMORIES" I will always treasure—a wealth of values I have collected over the years to be brought out now and then in reminiscence.

O Is for the "OBSTACLES" she helped me hurdle. If I was sad, she smiled, and my spirit rose. Behold, the sun shone once again, and I was warm.

T Is for the "TIME" she so willingly gives. How often she feels my sorrows and pain, and eases my insecurities; wrapping her child in love; instilling faith in the Father; conveying understanding of God's Word.

H Is for the "HAPPINESS" she brings into my life filled with the Spirit of God flowing from her to me. A heart-felt hug and kiss showing she is proud of me and making me know that I am wanted and needed.

E Is for the "ENDLESS" love, boundless without effort; a love so deeply embedded in her heart and fused into mine. Through her love and faith she teaches me to love others.

R Is for the "RAPTURE" with which I bask in her care. Respect still permeates with ease, and joy still resonates from her heart to mine, even across the miles. I pray to God that she knows her child loves her.

She has endeared herself to me!
If only every child could have a mother such as her.
Keep her in Your care and watch over her possessively, Dear God.

"A Mother's Love" is dedicated to the memory of Lydia Middlestead and Lillian Monson and to all children who love their mothers and to all mothers who love their children.

John 19:26-27
26 When Jesus therefore saw His mother, and the disciple whom He loved standing by, He said to His mother, "Woman, behold your son!" 27 Then He said to the disciple, "Behold your mother!" And from that hour that disciple took her to his own *home*.

A MOTHER'S LOVE
by W. Monson

Our Father in heaven,
Whose love is divine,
Thanks for the love
Of a mother like mine.
And in Thy great mercy
Look down from above
And grant this mother
The gift of Your love.
Then all through the years
Whatever betides her
Assure her each day
That You are beside her.
And Father in heaven
Show me the ways,
To lighten her tasks
And brighten her days.
And bless her dear heart
With the insight to see,
That her love means more
Than this whole world to me.

"Faith" is dedicated to Pastor Gary Hooper of the Family Worship Center in Fargo, North Dakota and to his devoted wife, Melodee. They are purposely and soulfully called by God to pray for others as they share the power of prayer and the good news of the saving grace of God, His Son, Jesus Christ.

Matthew 24:14
[14] And this gospel of the kingdom will be preached in all the world as a witness to all the nations, and then the end will come.

Ephesians 2:8-10
[8] For by grace you have been saved through faith, and that not of yourselves; *it is* the gift of God, [9] not of works, lest anyone should boast. [10] For we are His workmanship, created in Christ Jesus for good works, which God prepared beforehand that we should walk in them.

FAITH
by W. Monson

I wondered what it meant to be
Constantly in prayer.
I didn't know the meaning of
A faith that we must share.

But when I opened up my heart
And let the Holy Spirit in,
He cast the devil out of me
And washed away my sin.

I know that Jesus died for me
Upon that blood stained cross.
He washed me in His precious blood,
That my soul would not be lost.

I must tell the precious story
Of God's holy love and care,
For others who may hear it
And come to God in prayer.

"Jesus, My Light" is dedicated to those who are following the path that Jesus created for us to come out of the worldly fear of pain and death.

1 Corinthians 1:4-8
[4] I thank my God always concerning you for the grace of God which was given to you by Christ Jesus, [5] that you were enriched in everything by Him in all utterance and all knowledge, [6] even as the testimony of Christ was confirmed in you, [7] so that you come short in no gift, eagerly waiting for the revelation of our Lord Jesus Christ, [8] who will also confirm you to the end, *that you may be* blameless in the day of our Lord Jesus Christ.

JESUS, MY LIGHT
by C. Erwin

Oh, Lord of life, who died for me,
Open my eyes that I may see,
The love that lasts eternally,
Can only come from God.

Too long I followed Satan's path,
Avenged myself by grudge and wrath.
Then Jesus brought me into faith.
I died. He gave me life.

Oh, death to sin and shame, how sweet!
New life, God gives with each heartbeat.
I laid my sins at Jesus' feet.
He washed them all away.

With joy and peace He filled my soul.
His loving touch my heart made whole.
To serve Him always is my goal,
My refuge and my stay.

Oh, Lamb, who is the sinner's light,
With robe the white of purest white,
Who makes the darkest darkness bright,
Oh, light my path for me.

"His Blood, His Joy" is dedicated to Charles and Toni Reinke, Rifle, Colorado, who have faith in the new covenant from God.

Hebrews 12:1-2
[1] Therefore we also, since we are surrounded by so great a cloud of witnesses, let us lay aside every weight, and the sin which so easily ensnares *us*, and let us run with endurance the race that is set before us, [2] looking unto Jesus, the author and finisher of *our* faith, who for the joy that was set before Him endured the cross, despising the shame, and has sat down at the right hand of the throne of God.

HIS BLOOD, HIS JOY
by W. Monson

His blood!
His blood!
His precious blood,
Poured from His human veins.
To know Him and to understand
Surpasses worldly gains.
He gives the grace of calming peace,
Amid the strife that will not cease.
He fills me with His joy!
Oh, He fills me with His joy!
When one day, my race is run,
And by His grace the prize due won,
No more will pain and sorrow be,
Nor Satan bother me.
I'll bow down at His feet in praise,
My song be for unending days.
I'll thank Him for the joy!
Oh, I'll thank Him for the joy!

"Calmed" is dedicated to Stevie Shapley, Jr., Lewis Renfro, III, David Stone, Jr., Malachi Stone, James Renfro, Kayden Renfro, and to all young boys who are blessings from God.

James 3:17-18
17 But the wisdom that comes from heaven is first of all pure; then peace-loving, considerate, submissive, full of mercy and good fruit, impartial and sincere. 18 Peacemakers who sow in peace reap a harvest of righteousness.

CALMED
by C. Erwin

Holy Spirit,
Grace Devine,
Search this sinful
Heart of mine.
Fill me with
Your loving peace.
All my sin
Of worry cease.
All my grumbling
Bring to end.
Thou my guide,
My faithful friend.
To the cross
My burden call.
Hold me, Spirit,
Lest I fall.

Amen.

"God, You are Everything" is dedicated to Tiffany and Miracle Renfro, from Casa Grande, Arizona. May the love and grace of God flow through their lives.

Matthew 19:14
14 But Jesus said, "Let the little children come to Me, and do not forbid them; for of such is the kingdom of heaven."

John 1:12-13
12 But as many as received Him, to them He gave the right to become children of God, to those who believe in His name: 13 who were born, not of blood, nor of the will of the flesh, nor of the will of man, but of God.

GOD, YOU ARE EVERYTHING
by M. Monson

You are everything I could want or need.
You are the author of my mind.
You have planned my future days ahead,
And the past I left behind.

(Refrain)
God, You are everything.
God, You are everything.
God, You are everything.
You are everything to me.

You are The Avenger of the wicked.
You are the council of the wise.
You have placed the glowing spark of life
In the little children's eyes.
(Repeat Refrain)

You are the defender
Of the righteous.
You are the wind
That sweeps the sky.
You have taught the languages to men,
And the words that they apply.
(Repeat Refrain)

GOD, YOU ARE EVERYTHING (Continued...)

You are the mightiest of the mighty.
You are the strongest of the strong.
You have formed the farthest galaxy,
And the earth I walk upon.
(Repeat Refrain)

You are the grandest
And most glorious.
You are the love that will not end.
You are the Alpha and Omega,
And You are my God and friend.
(Repeat Refrain)

Truthful Gems

Psalm 31:14
14 But as for me, I trust in You, O LORD;
    I say, "You *are* my God."

Proverbs 17:27
27 He who has knowledge spares his words,
    And a man of understanding is of a calm spirit.

Proverbs 30:5
5 Every word of God *is* pure;
    He *is* a shield to those who put their trust in Him.

2 Peter 1:16
16 For we did not follow cunningly devised fables when we made known to you the power and coming of our Lord Jesus Christ, but were eyewitnesses of His majesty.

1 John 3:2
2 Beloved, now we are children of God; and it has not yet been revealed what we shall be, but we know that when He is revealed, we shall be like Him, for we shall see Him as He is.

"Just Say Jesus" is dedicated to all who have called upon the name of Jesus.

Matthew 18:10-11
[10] "Take heed that you do not despise one of these little ones, for I say to you that in heaven their angels always see the face of My Father who is in heaven. [11] For the Son of Man has come to save that which was lost.[a]

Luke 8:39
[39] "Return to your own house, and tell what great things God has done for you." And he went his way and proclaimed throughout the whole city what great things Jesus had done for him.

JUST SAY JESUS
by M. Monson

I could hear the devil growling from underneath my feet,
A harsh and raspy roaring of badgering deceit.
He thought he had me in his foothold grip to kill,
To become a horror fear-filled demon,
A captive of his will.

Then just one silent word caused the devil to retreat.
From inside a breathless void my heart began to beat.
My life is saved by His Word God has shared with us.
I will be forever thankful for that Word.
His name is Jesus.

Although the demons mutter, stutter, clank, and clatter.
Although the devil prowls around, it does not matter.
When I call Jesus, angels' faces appear near,
And all the clamor of the devil
And his demons disappear.

Up above a garland of angels blanket the skies,
Gazing down from the heavens
With love light-filtered eyes.
With faith I see angels and believe what I see.
They are the guardians of God's children
Watching us carefully.

"Oh, Dear Lord of Light" is dedicated to Roy, Jr. and Melissa Renfro, Tonopah, Nevada, who carry the light of the Lord in their lives.

Isaiah 60:19
¹⁹ " The sun shall no longer be your light by day,
   Nor for brightness shall the moon give light to you;
   But the LORD will be to you an everlasting light,
   And your God your glory.

Acts 4:33
³³ And with great power the apostles gave witness to the resurrection of the Lord Jesus. And great grace was upon them all.

OH, DEAR LORD OF LIGHT
by W. Monson

Oh, Dear Lord of Light,
Who has come to give life,
Whom it pleased, a servant to be.
By Your grace and Your power,
Help me to do right.
Help me to be who
You want me to be.

The life that I live,
Is the life that You give.
No man in his mind can conceive
A love, that poured out Your blood,
Each sinner to save.
All that You ask in return,
Is believe.

I give you my heart,
Lest from Thee I would part,
My life would be useless and cold.
Send forth Your Holy Spirit
To guide all my steps.
My feet will not stray away from Your fold.

King of creation,
Hear my supplication,
For all who are so dear to me.
Send pure joy into them
That Your Spirit brings.
Help them to be who You want them to be.

"Gap Rappers' Rap" is dedicated to Jacob Lowell Renfro, a Christian rapper, witness, and leader. This rap is dedicated to the Christian rapping ministries that are called by God to be involved in the Great Commission.

Ezekiel 22:30
30 So I sought for a man among them who would make a wall, and stand in the gap before Me on behalf of the land, that I should not destroy it; but I found no one.

Ephesians 6:13-16
13 Therefore take up the whole armor of God, that you may be able to withstand in the evil day, and having done all, to stand.
14 Stand therefore, having girded your waist with truth, having put on the breastplate of righteousness, 15 and having shod your feet with the preparation of the gospel of peace;
16 above all, taking the shield of faith with which you will be able to quench all the fiery darts of the wicked one.

GAP RAPPERS' RAP
by M. Monson

We stand in the light in the gap.
We stand to the right of the wrong.
We are the Gap Rappers!
We are the fish snappers!
We are the demon trappers.

We are armed with the armor
And the sword of the Lord.
This is where we belong!
This is where you come on!
Come on! Come on!
We are the bold and the strong.
With the battle cry
For the spiritual poor,
We are blazing in the realm
Of the spiritual war.
We hold the Holy Ghost force
Of the Power on High,
With the promise of life
That will never die!

GAP RAPPERS' RAP (Continued...)

Hook:
That is why we are saved.
We are saved from the grave.
From without to within
We will track you down.
We will back you up.
We will pull you in,
So you begin again.
I am a Parable Chimer.
I am a Mountain Mover.
I am a Vision Leader.
I am a Foe Defeater.

Chorus:
We have the Book.
You took the hook.
The hook is the Book.
It is the Word of God
With the Covenant
And the Testament
Is to testify
That the Son He sent
Is a true event.

GAP RAPPERS' RAP (Continued...)

We flow by the grace
Of the Heavenly Host.
We flow by the power
Of the Holy Ghost.
We are witnesses for the cross.
We are prayer warriors for the lost.
We are in a Christian charge
On a mighty mission,
In a Christian charge
In the Great Commission.
We are commissioned by Christ.
He conquered death.
He conquered sin.
We challenge the world to enter in!

We carry the Word.
We carry the meek.
We are the message of hope.
We are the message you seek!
We pitch our tents by the sea of glass,
To call the weak and to claim the flash.
(Repeat Hook and Chorus)

GAP RAPPERS' RAP (Continued...)

We stand on the rim
By the pit of the mire.
Our goal is to pull you out of the fire,
Where the devil and his demons
With their lies and by scheming
Have tied you up!
They have captured you,
With debauchery and mockery.
With slivery shock and misery.

With the evil eyes of the demons' stare,
They think that they can keep you there,
With the prince of air!
He is the grim reaper!
He is the night creeper!
In the bottom of the pit!
Do not believe it!
Do not believe it!
We are the army of liberty.
We are called to victory.
Our faith is Calvary.
God set us free!
(Repeat Hook and Chorus)

GAP RAPPERS' RAP (Continued...)

We have come
To stomp the footsteps on the stair.
Stop the whispers in the air.
Block the darts of the enemy.
Break the walls of hostility.
Christ set you free!
He loves your soul!
He will not let you go!
He will not let you go!

We are here to wake you up
From the nap of the dead.
We stand between life and death
Inside your heart
And outside your head.
We are the chalk. We are the block.
We are the breath. We are the talk.

We are the Gap Rappers!
We are the fish snappers!
We are the demon trappers!
(Repeat Hook and Chorus)

"Biblical Maturity" is dedicated to Christians who are searching through the scriptures for direction in their lives.

1 Corinthians 12:7-11
7 But the manifestation of the Spirit is given to each one for the profit *of all:* 8 for to one is given the word of wisdom through the Spirit, to another the word of knowledge through the same Spirit, 9 to another faith by the same Spirit, to another gifts of healings by the same[b] Spirit, 10 to another the working of miracles, to another prophecy, to another discerning of spirits, to another *different* kinds of tongues, to another the interpretation of tongues. 11 But one and the same Spirit works all these things, distributing to each one individually as He wills.

BIBLICAL MATURITY
by M. Monson

There was
A deep and dark hole
Rolling down
Behind me.
Demon eyes were on the
Wall,
Glowing when they found
Me.
Drifting, air-blown
Spirits were pushing up
Against me.

Smiling, although
Anguished
And rising,
Nearly languished,
Shielding my soul,
I held the Bible out
Before me.
Wielding God's living Word,
No spirit could
Ignore me.

Witnessing
Everywhere
I went,
To some, I was God sent.

Dodging and scrambling
For spiritual
Proximity,
I know that I raced
Diabolical
Atrocity.

Having sinned deliberately,
I opened up the pit.
By showing faith in God,
The demons fell back into it.

There are spiritual gifts
That are given to
Each one.
When we understand
Jesus is the Lord,
And God's Son.
First Corinthians Twelve
Gives me this security.
Unbound,
On solid ground,
With Biblical
Maturity.

"Heaven's Little Angels" is dedicated to Leonna Chavoya, Tucson, Arizona, a woman who has a heart filled with love for little children and other people on this earth.

Proverbs 31:29-31
[29] " Many daughters have done well,
But you excel them all."
[30] Charm *is* deceitful and beauty *is* passing,
But a woman *who* fears the LORD, she shall be praised.
[31] Give her of the fruit of her hands,
And let her own works praise her in the gates.

Matthew 18:5
[5] Whoever receives one little child like this in My name receives Me.

HEAVEN'S LITTLE ANGELS
by M. Monson

A kind man once asked me,
"Why do children have to die?"
I told him,
"Heaven's little angels
Are sledding in the sky.
They are happy waving from the clouds
To show
Their earthly parents walking by below
That they would never ever want to go
Back down to earth again,
Oh, no!"

"I Thank You, Lord" is dedicated to Rick and Kay Burkhardt, Sioux Falls, South Dakota, who pray for and lead others to an understanding of the merciful message of the Lord Jesus Christ.

Mark 11:23-24
**23 For assuredly, I say to you, whoever says to this mountain, 'Be removed and be cast into the sea,' and does not doubt in his heart, but believes that those things he says will be done, he will have whatever he says.
24 Therefore I say to you, whatever things you ask when you pray, believe that you receive *them,* and you will have *them.***

I THANK YOU, LORD
by W. Monson

I thank you, Lord, for sending those
Who lifted up
Your bloodstained cross,
Until my blinded eyes could see
That sinful pleasure is but loss.

I thank you, Lord, as years went by,
Whene'er my faith and trust did wane,
You sent someone to reach a hand,
To bring me back to trust again.

Someone
Who humbly bowed their head,
And on their bended knees did pray
To send Your Spirit in my heart,
Filled with the light
That leads my way.
Amen.

"Love So Pure, So Free" is dedicated to Seth Erwin, who promotes the truth that we are all set free from the bondage of sin by the wondrous love of the Lord God.

Ephesians 2:13
13 But now in Christ Jesus you who once were far off have been brought near by the blood of Christ.

LOVE SO PURE, SO FREE
by W. Monson

As I look out my window, Lord, I see Your loving care.
I see Your beauty 'round about,
Of things You want to share.
At times they go unnoticed though
As sin and self combine,
And blinded eyes just cannot see Your glory so divine.

Your grace You give abundantly,
I cannot comprehend
A love that is so pure, so free,
And steadfast to the end.
You gave Your precious Son to die
To pay the price of sin.
You make the vilest sinner clean
And bid him to come in.

You only ask a contrite heart,
Though filled with sin and shame,
Then wash him in the cleansing blood,
And take away the blame.
I'm awed to think a Holy God
Who made both earth and sky,
Should care so much to stoop and lift
A sinner such as I.

"Loving Grace" is dedicated to James and Patti Hildebrant and Richard and Jeanie Hass, of Valley City, North Dakota, and their children. The Word of God is carried by knowledge within their minds and by love inside their hearts.

Ephesians 5:1-2
1 Therefore be imitators of God as dear children. 2 And walk in love, as Christ also has loved us and given Himself for us, an offering and a sacrifice to God for a sweet-smelling aroma.

LOVING GRACE
by W. Monson and C. Erwin

Deep in my heart
There is a stir,
Where no
Human eye
Can see.
Your Holy Word,
Oh Lord, I hear,
For my child, you too,
The cross must bear,
And others'
Burdens share,
If you would follow me.

Unspeakable,
The sorrow great,
As sinner on
His knees doth fall,
The Holy Spirit still will wait,
The Shepherd stands
Nearby the gate,
Although the hour is late,
For answer to His call.

What wondrous joy
Of loving grace,
Jesus, His forgiveness speaks.
No worldly pleasure
Can replace,
When I behold the Savior's face.
I have run the victor's race,
My soul
His glory seeks.

I do not know,
I can not tell,
How the arm
Of God - therein
Reaches down to the
Depths of hell
And breaks the spell
Where sinner fell.
The Savior of my soul
Yes, I will follow Him.

"Fulfilled" is dedicated to Nevaeh Stone, a young woman with a big heart who is seeking the will of God in the daily activities of her life.

Deuteronomy 26:17
17 Today you have proclaimed the LORD to be your God, and that you will walk in His ways and keep His statutes, His commandments, and His judgments, and that you will obey His voice.

John 17:13
13 But now I come to You, and these things I speak in the world, that they may have My joy fulfilled in themselves.

FULFILLED
by C. Erwin

I sought
The world over
For worldly pleasure,
And found my want
Grow ever greater.
Nothing I ventured
As days went by,
Could fulfill
Nor satisfy.

Then I looked beyond
This world to see
The Mountains
Great and high.
There a vision
Came to Raise,
The One to worship
And to praise.
Not made of silver
Nor of gold
Despised and lowly
To behold.

A bleeding form
Upon a cross,
Dying for
The sinful...lost.

Crying out in pain, alone,
"Father, forgive them.
They are mine.
Grant them grace
To worship you.
For
They do not know
What they do."

The dawning light
That filled my soul
The cleansing blood
That made me whole.

Oh, risen Lord,
Control my will.
My lowly cup
With service fill.
My pleasure now
I find in Thee
Oh, Holy Lord
Of Calvary.

"The Dark Hour" is dedicated to Kathy Riehle, Kiowa, Colorado, who has by the Spirit of the Lord seen others suffer through darkness and thus is intent on helping them step into the light of salvation.

Isaiah 50:10
10 " Who among you fears the LORD?
   Who obeys the voice of His Servant?
   Who walks in darkness
   And has no light?
   Let him trust in the name of the LORD
   And rely upon his God.

THE DARK HOUR
by W. Monson

Oh, hear me Lord, Dear Lord, my God,
As through this darkness now, I plod.
My heart is heavy like the sod.
Guide me, precious Jesus.

As I cry out in grief and pain,
I'm filled with dark clouds of the rain.
Help me to rise and laugh again.
Bring light, precious Jesus.

My soul is heavy with this load.
So rough and rugged is the road.
I've reaped the thorns that sin has sown.
Help me, precious Jesus.

I had heard my child laugh and play,
It seems it was but yesterday.
Then if young feet have gone astray.
Gather them, Dear Jesus.

My voice to Thee, Oh, Lord, I raise.
Fill up my lips with grateful praise,
That I may serve Thee all my days,
Thankfully, Dear Jesus.

"God's Love for Me" is dedicated to Beverly Joy, Wellborn, Texas, whose heart is committed to Jesus Christ through the knowledge that Jesus died as God's sacrifice for the redemption of all people.

1 Corinthians 5:7
7 Therefore purge out the old leaven, that you may be a new lump, since you truly are unleavened. For indeed Christ, our Passover, was sacrificed for us.[c]

GOD'S LOVE FOR ME
by W. Monson

I cried out to God one night,
"Why can't I have my way!"
I wrestled with the Spirit
'Til it was nearly day.
Oh, how strong the love of sin,
Then as the sun came up,
It was me,
myself, and I
Who sought
Full measure of the cup.

God led me to a lonely hill,
Where stood a blood-stained,
Wooden cross.
I gazed upon the form that hung,
And cried,
"It's Christ who paid the cost!"

The crown of thorns upon His head.
His red blood gushing from the tear.
I bowed my head in anguished shame.
I knew my sins had hung Him there.

GOD'S LOVE FOR ME (Continued...)

Then I cried out to God again,
"Take away this thirst for sinning.
Show me how to live for you.
"Help me make a new beginning.
With love-filled eyes, He looked at me,
Despite the grief, the blood, the pain.
I gave to Him my contrite heart.
His blood had washed
Away the stain.

Upon the ground, I fell and wept,
"Why, oh why, all this for me?"
I am not worthy, precious Lord,
That You should die to set me free."

I heard a voice,
"Not you alone,
So go and tell your brother.
The Son of God has shed his blood
That all should love each other."

Oh, now the joy! The living joy!
That overflows my soul.
I know the very grace of God
Alone has made me whole.

Truthful Gems

Deuteronomy 6:5
⁵ You shall love the LORD your God with all your heart, with all your soul, and with all your strength.

John 14:23
²³ Jesus answered and said to him, "If anyone loves Me, he will keep My word; and My Father will love him, and We will come to him and make Our home with him.

Romans 8:39
³⁹ nor height nor depth, nor any other created thing, shall be able to separate us from the love of God which is in Christ Jesus our Lord.

Ephesians 6:24
²⁴ Grace *be* with all those who love our Lord Jesus Christ in sincerity. Amen.

1 John 5:1
¹ Whoever believes that Jesus is the Christ is born of God, and everyone who loves Him who begot also loves him who is begotten of Him.

"True Friendship" is dedicated to Jenny Perkins, Gainesville, Florida, a woman who knows the greatest friend of all, Jesus Christ, the Son of God and the Savior of those who believe in Him.

Proverbs 18:24

24 **A man** *who has* **friends must himself be friendly,**[b]

   But there is a friend *who* **sticks closer than a brother.**

TRUE FRIENDSHIP
by W. Monson

I judged a friend today, Dear Lord,
Then what did I found out?
It wasn't she who spread
That gossip all about.

But in my heart, I did accuse
That one whom I call friend,
And angry thoughts
Began to bring
Our friendship
To an end.

We oft' insist a thing is true
Before we do find out,
Or fail to give the other one,
The benefit of doubt.

Oh, thank You, Lord,
For helping me
My errs
In time to know,
Before I broke
A precious heart
By letting
Anger grow.

"Oh, God, Keep My Heart" is dedicated to Edna Middlestead, Fargo, North Dakota, who gives to others without thinking of the cost.

John 12:3
³ Then Mary took a pound of very costly oil of spikenard, anointed the feet of Jesus, and wiped His feet with her hair. And the house was filled with the fragrance of the oil.

OH, GOD, KEEP MY HEART
by C. Erwin

Oh, God, keep my heart from evil desire,
And my lips from speaking deceit.
   Help me depart where sin enters in,
   Seeking Your guidance to stay in the right
   Imploring my footsteps to walk in the light,
     As humbly I kneel at Your feet.

     My days without God, I put far from me.
        Oh, joy, just to walk in His way!
      Searching to know His love and His will,
Yielding my mind, understanding His word,
   Looking behind, I can no longer afford,
      No longer my footsteps will stray.

     Your sacrifice, Jesus, the blood You shed,
       The price that You paid for my sin.
     Though Satan taunts to lead me astray,
     My heart and my life will ever be Thine,
I place them, Dear Lord, in Your hands so divine.
       The race that I run, help me win.

     Soon the power of sin defeated will be,
       My spirit rejoicing will soar,
      And His beauty so great I behold,
    Praises to Jesus, my Savior, I'll sing,
    As I see the face of my Heavenly King,
   When death comes to knock at my door.

"The Guest" is dedicated to people who are alone and without family here on earth, but who will one day see their family in heaven.

Matthew 9:36
36 But when He saw the multitudes, He was moved with compassion for them, because they were weary[b] and scattered, like sheep having no shepherd.

Jude 1:21
21 keep yourselves in the love of God, looking for the mercy of our Lord Jesus Christ unto eternal life.

THE GUEST
by W. Monson, C. Erwin, and M. Monson

Oh, precious Lord,
Help me through the tragedy
Of my own self-seeking quest.
You see me,
An earthly sinner - as I am,
Yet You call me Your honored guest.

The Good Shepherd,
Leading Your sheep You came to claim
Our sacrificial pain
Earning men's atonement,
With Your Holy Name.
You broke the yoke of sinful blame.

My entrance into faith
Is not a task…but grace.
In humble prayer, I ask,
Your forgiveness, unsurpassed.
This guest You called
Is in Your care
And home at last.

"God Whispers" is dedicated to Connie Nichols, Camden, Arkansas, who has initiated the love of the Lord Jesus within the family and continues to encourage and support others with prayer.

1 John 4:7-11

7 Beloved, let us love one another, for love is of God; and everyone who loves is born of God and knows God. 8 He who does not love does not know God, for God is love. 9 In this the love of God was manifested toward us, that God has sent His only begotten Son into the world, that we might live through Him. 10 In this is love, not that we loved God, but that He loved us and sent His Son *to be* the propitiation for our sins. 11 Beloved, if God so loved us, we also ought to love one another.

GOD WHISPERS
by W. Monson and M. Monson

With sorrowing soul and aching heart,
I see my brother's pain and fear.
"Oh, Jesus, help him, Lord," I cry
He whispers, "I am standing here."

Dark shadowy grief
A silent breath,
I hear my father's dying sigh.
"Oh, Jesus, help him, Lord, I beg."
He whispers, "I am standing by."

Small whimpering sound
And shaking sob,
My sister's weeping voice I hear.
"Merciful Lord, please comfort her."
He whispers, "I am standing near."

And wavering not,
She kneels in prayer.
She asks the Lord, "What must I do?"
My mother's faith has taught us well.
He whispers, "My child, I love you."

"Dear Lord, help me
Embrace my family,
With mind and heart and helping hand."
My mother's prayers have taught me love.
He whispers, "Child, you understand."

"Lord" is dedicated to those who share the Word of God and express their faith to others.

1 John 2:25
²⁵ And this is the promise that He has promised us—eternal life.

Revelations 2:17
¹⁷ "He who has an ear, let him hear what the Spirit says to the churches. To him who overcomes I will give some of the hidden manna to eat. And I will give him a white stone, and on the stone a new name written which no one knows except him who receives *it*.'"

LORD
by M. Monson

Lord, let me not forsake
My first love for You.
Give me the will to do
Whatever you would
Have me to.
Keep me faithful even
To the point of death,
Until You share with me
An everlasting new life breath.

Lord, let me long remain
True unto Your call.
From my sins I lament and
Repent of them all.
Come to me and help me
Practice to believe.
Give me my new name
Upon the white stone
That I receive.

Lord, let me heed
Your Word
With reverent deeds.
Give me the need
To move in love
And plant Your seeds.
Then, unto the end,
Lord, keep me as You are,
That I will overcome
And hold Your shining
Morning star.

Lord, call my name
When You wake me from
The dead.
I remember what I received
And what You said.
You have
Promised
You will not
Leave me behind.
Refine me,
Wretched, pitiful, poor,
Naked, and blind.

"In the Light of the Spirit" is dedicated to those who have given their burdens of life to Jesus to carry.

Psalm 27:1
¹ The LORD *is* my light and my salvation;
    Whom shall I fear?
    The LORD *is* the strength of my life;
    Of whom shall I be afraid?

IN THE LIGHT OF THE SPIRIT
by W. Monson

I drove home in the fog the other morn.
It was so dark, fearful, and forlorn.
Only dense shadows did appear.
One step ahead I could not see,
Until the dawn,
When the light broke through.
Then everything was clear to me.

I walked in fog along life's weary way.
It became more frightening every day.
The Holy Spirit spoke to me,
"Christ Jesus died for even you."
With the dawn the darkness fell away.
God's love for me came shining through.

Oh, we who bear the heavy load of sin,
Struggling where to turn,
Without - within.
Lord Jesus calls, "Come with me.
I will carry your heavy load."
Unto the world God sent His own Son,
He paid the price of sin we owed.

"The End" is dedicated to all believers.

Isaiah 24:20
**20 The earth shall reel to and fro like a drunkard,
And shall totter like a hut;
Its transgression shall be heavy upon it,
And it will fall, and not rise again.**

Revelation 5:11-12
**11 Then I looked, and I heard the voice of many angels around the throne, the living creatures, and the elders; and the number of them was ten thousand times ten thousand, and thousands of thousands, 12 saying with a loud voice:
" Worthy is the Lamb who was slain
To receive power and riches and wisdom,
And strength and honor and glory and blessing!"**

Revelation 6:14
14 Then the sky receded as a scroll when it is rolled up, and every mountain and island was moved out of its place.

THE END
by M. Monson

The trumpet above will sound the call.
The mountain tops will crumble and fall.
The throne on high will rumble and peal.
The earth will rock and reel.

    Ten thousand times ten thousand
    Of angels will sing.
    All the earth and the sea and
    The heavens will ring.

Lighting flashes will shimmer and lash.
Crumbling mountains will melt like wax.
Bright, glimmering stars will fall and crash.
He is the first and last.

    The beginning and the end.
    The great God, I Am.
    The beginning and the end.
    Oh, my God, here I am.

Then we will stand in a grander domain.
We will remain in His Holy name.
Praising the Son of God who came,
And will forever reign.

    Honor and praise to the Lamb.
    He came to be slain.
    Honor and praise to the Lamb.
    He is always the same.

THE END (Continued...)

He will lead the triumphant procession,
Compelling us up to redemption.
He will rule in jeweled reception,
    The Magnificent One.

Oh come, Most Excellent Son.
    Magnificent One.
Oh come, Most Excellent Son,
    The Magnificent One.

The believers will hear the angel say,
That there should no longer be delay.
Then the old order will pass away.
    He will capture His clay.

Oh, my Dear God, help me go.
    As soon I will flow.
Oh, my Dear God, help me go,
    As I upwardly flow.

The sky above will roll up like a scroll.
The golden streets of heaven will show.
His feet like burnished bronze will glow.
    He will rapture my soul.

Oh, my Lord God Almighty,
    Shining so brightly.
Oh, my Lord God Almighty,
    Is shining so brightly.

Truthful Gems

Psalm 90:12
12 So teach *us* to number our days,
   That we may gain a heart of wisdom.

Mark 11:25
25 "And whenever you stand praying, if you have anything against anyone, forgive him, that your Father in heaven may also forgive you your trespasses.

1 Corinthians 3:16
16 Do you not know that you are the temple of God and *that* the Spirit of God dwells in you?

Romans 12:21
21 *Do not be overcome by evil, but overcome evil with good.*

Romans 15:13
13 Now may the God of hope fill you with all joy and peace in believing, that you may abound in hope by the power of the Holy Spirit.

AUTHOR'S BIO.

C. Erwin has always had a zest for God avidly demonstrated by her sincere love for humanity and the living world God created. She attributes her caring spirit to the consistency of her parent's biblical sharing of the Word of God along with the example of their own love given to her, to friends, to neighbors, and even to the wondering vagabond. C. Erwin has a heart-warming motto she lives by. She has open arms. If she catches you off-guard, you might suddenly receive a discerning, comfortable hug that speaks a thousand words of how much you are appreciated. Ask anyone who knows her. They will tell you.

Growing up with three brothers and the middle sister of three sisters, she was outstanding in gymnastics, drama, choir, and band. Her solo performances in voice are remembered in numerous church choirs, local and state school choruses, and as gracious favors at funerals, weddings, and birthdays. People often request her songs.

C. Erwin's musical talent is a blessing from God that she has continued to bless others with. If you have the opportunity to come to North Dakota and meet her, you can believe she will find the opportunity to give you a hug. Then, when you hear her sing, you will never forget her voice. If you have read the words in this book, you will have heard her expressions of love and nearly almost heard her sing. Now, come and listen and get your hug.

If you can not come here to North Dakota, you can take the advice of C. Erwin, and give this book a hug.

AUTHOR'S BIO.

M. Monson loves the Lord and will tell you so. She is an author, artist, and music composer eager to put her talents to work for the purpose of demonstrating the love of Jesus.

According to M. Monson all the dedications, the poems, and the art in this book were truly inspired by the Holy Spirit. The dedications are examples of words of encouragement to any and all the churches that preach and teach that the Lord Jesus Christ is the Savior of sinners. The dedications in both the books are to the churches and people who have in some way personally touched her life, a member of her family's life, or the life of a friend.

M. Monson's dad was her hero and her mother her heroine. She would like to tell all fathers and mothers that the most important thing they can do for their children is to give them the knowledge of the Bible. The Bible can give hope to the hopeless, strength to the weak, and the answers to life's most difficult questions. When you hand your child a bible, you hand them the gift of life.

As a testimony of how the Lord Jesus Christ touches others, M. Monson says she wants everyone to understand that Jesus is seeking them for eternity. She knows that Jesus will touch everyone who asks Him to come into their heart.

Then, because M. Monson believes that the Vine of Christ is within all the churches who proclaim Jesus as the Son of God, she encourages everyone to listen to the voice of the man of God, your pastor or reverend. God is listening, too.

www.ingramcontent.com/pod-product-compliance
Lightning Source LLC
Chambersburg PA
CBHW041511220426
43661CB00047B/1531